D0773924

**SELECT EDITIONS**

"Everything's a circle
We're each responsible for
our own actions.
It will come back."
Betty Laverdure, Ojibway.

ISBN: 1 86476 013 3

Copyright © Axiom Publishers,
This printing Select Editions, 1999

# Lasting Friendship

illustrations:
JAN GALLEHAWK

calligraphy:
JIM BILLINGSLEY

A friend is a gift you give yourself

English Proverb

A good
feeling
gets even
better
when its
shared.

Better
to be alone
than in bad
company.

The more you give, the more you get;
The more you laugh-the less you fret;
The more you do unselfishly
The more you live abundantly.
The more of everything you share
The more you'll always have to spare;
That life is good, and friends are kind.
For only what we give away
Enriches us from day to day.

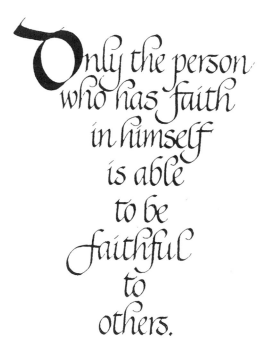

Only the person
who has faith
in himself
is able
to be
faithful
to
others.

Things will
probably
come out right,

But sometimes
it takes strong
nerves
just to watch.

The quickest way
to get what you want
is to help others get
what they want.

A friendship
founded on
business
is better than
a business
founded on
friendship.

a real friend
never gets in
your way,
-unless you
happen to
be on the
way
down.

*Friendship*
*is a plant*
*which must*
*be often watered*

meeting interesting
people depends less
on where you go
than who you are.

The proper office
of a friend is to
side with you
when you are
wrong.
Nearly anybody
will side with you
when you are
right.

Mark Twain

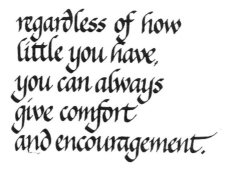

regardless of how
little you have,
you can always
give comfort
and encouragement.

We do not mind
our not arriving
anywhere nearly
as much as our
not having any
company on the
way

Frank Moore Colby

In great matters
men show themselves
as they wish to be
seen; in small matters,
as they are.

# Take Time

TAKE TIME FOR FRIENDSHIP WHICH YOU CAN,
THE HOURS FLY SWIFTLY, AND THE NEED
THAT PRESSES ON YOUR FELLOWMAN
MAY FADE AWAY AT EQUAL SPEED,
AND YOU MAY SIGH BEFORE THE END
THAT YOU HAVE FAILED TO PLAY THE FRIEND

NOT ALL LIFE'S PRIDE IS BORN OF FAME,
NOT ALL THE JOY OF WORK IS WON,
TOO LATE WE HANG OUR HEADS IN SHAME,
REMEMBERING THE GOOD WE COULD HAVE DONE;
TOO LATE WE WISH THAT WE HAD STAYED
TO COMFORT THOSE WHO CALLED FOR AID.

*Edgar A. Guest*

IT IS THE
SECOND WORD
THAT
MAKES
A QUARREL.

*Japanese
Proverb.*

relationship? It's never too late to heal an injured

Kind words
like good deeds
are eternal,
you never know
where their
influence
will end.

your friend
is the person
who knows all about
you
&
still likes you.

My best friend
is my teddy bear,
he never tells
my secrets.

Hospitality
consists in
a little fire,
a little food
and an
immense
quiet.

It's great to say 'Good morning'
It's fine to say 'Hello,'
But better still to grasp the hand
Of a loyal friend you know.

A look may be forgotten;
A word misunderstood,
But touch of a human hand
Is a pledge of brotherhood.

Trust first in those
who say ~
"I made a mistake."

a smile is a
wrinkle that
shouldn't be
removed.

We share our happiness with each other—
and it becomes greater.

We share our troubles with each other
and they become smaller.

We share one another's griefs & burdens—
and their weight becomes possible to bear.

Learning
to
forgive
takes
practice.

It is by
forgiving
that
one is
forgiven.

*Mother Teresa*

*people are more
influenced by
how much you
care than by
how much
you know.*

The only way
to have a
friend is
to be one

Ralph Waldo Emerson

*Fire is the test
of gold,
adversity of
friendship.*

BETTER IS A FRIEND
THAT IS NEAR,

THAN A RELATIVE
FAR OFF.

If you stay focused
on yourself
you are guaranteed
to be miserable.

# Cheery~O!

If you smile the day will be cheery,
  If you smile the day will be bright.
If you think good thoughts you'll
                be happy,

And everything will work out
            just right.

So don't let a frown turn you sour,
  Don't let bad thoughts make
              you blue.

Just always remember, think
            positively,

For how you feel is up to you.

Susan L Wiener

If you see
someone
without a smile,
give them
one.

If you don't feel like
being pleasant, courteous
and kind, act that way
and the feelings will come.

Friendship
is like
wine
- the older
the better.

*To dislike yourself
is to insult
your friends.*

kindness is the
golden chain
by which
society is
bound
together.

The ornament
of a house is
the friends who
frequent it.

Emmerson

The most precious
of all possessions
is a wise and loyal
friend.

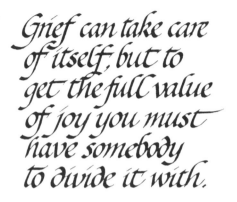

Grief can take care
of itself; but to
get the full value
of joy you must
have somebody
to divide it with.

Mark Twain

Be like the sun
and the meadow,

which are not in the
least concerned about
the coming winter.

If we live in peace
ourselves,
we in turn may
bring peace to others.

A peaceable man does more
good than a learned one.

Thomas A. Kempis

It's impossible
to accomplish
anything worthwhile
without the
help of other
people.

There is no better
exercise for the heart
than reaching
and lifting
someone
up.

Plotting revenge
only allows
the people who
hurt you
to hurt you
longer.

Being too quick to judge
someone can deprive you
of a great encounter and
the possibility of a
wonderful long-term
relationship.

# What to Count

Don't count how many years you've spent,
Just count the good you've done;
The times you've lent a helping hand,
The friends that you have won.
Count your deeds of kindness,
The smiles, not the tears;
Count all the pleasures that you've had,
But never count the years!

you can get
children
off your lap,

but you can never
get them out
of your heart.

a pessimist
is someone
who feels bad
~when she feels good
for fear
she will feel
worse
when she feels
better.

Someone gave me a smile today.

I tried my best to give it away
to everyone I chanced to meet,
as I walked down the street.

But everyone that I could see,
gave my smile right back to me.

When I got home, besides my
smile

I had enough to reach a mile.

*without
confidence
there is
no friendship.*

I expect to pass through life but once. If therefore, there can be any kindness I can show, or any good thing I can do for any fellow human being, let me do it now.
For I shall not pass this way again.

William Penn

We all have weaknesses.
But I have figured that
others have put up with
mine so tolerantly that
it would be less than fair
not to make a reasonable
discount for theirs.

do more than exist~ LIVE.
do more than touch~ FEEL.
do more than look~ SEE.
do more than hear~ LISTEN.
do more than talk~ SAY SOMETHING.

I am quick to count
others' offences
against me, but seldom
think about what
others suffer because of me.

I keep my friends
as misers do their
treasure, because
of all the things
granted by wisdom,
none is better than
a friendship.

Pietro Arentino

I'm not rich
and famous

But I do have

Priceless

grandchildren.

That friendship
will not
continue
to the end,
that is begun
for an end.

*Duty*
makes us do things well

but *Love* makes us do them
beautifully.

Rev. P. Brooks